PICTURE BOOK OF
REVOLUTIONARY WAR HEROES

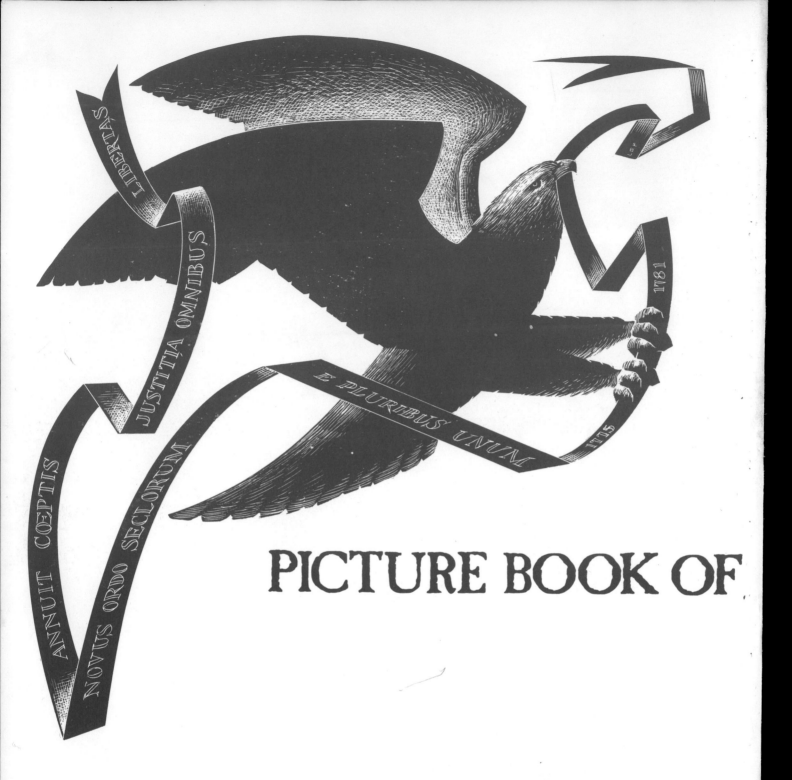

PICTURE BOOK OF

A Giniger Book
published in association with
STACKPOLE BOOKS

REVOLUTIONARY WAR HEROES

written and illustrated by

Leonard Everett Fisher

PICTURE BOOK OF REVOLUTIONARY WAR HEROES
Copyright © 1970 by
Leonard Everett Fisher
Published by
STACKPOLE BOOKS
Cameron and Kelker Streets
Harrisburg, Pa. 17105

ISBN 0-8117-1259-1
Library of Congress Catalog Card Number 70-123405

Printed in U.S.A.

INTRODUCTION

Early on the morning of April 19, 1775—the sun had not yet risen high enough into the sky to melt the cool ground mists of Massachusetts—a little line of Lexington militiamen stood on their town green and challenged the passage of a sizeable force of the British army. The British troops, part of a 700-man expedition from the Boston garrison, were bound for Concord on a mission of destruction. Their aim was to seize or destroy hidden stores of colonial arms before the Americans could use them in open rebellion against the government of King George III.

Outnumbered five to one or more, the stubborn, angry Americans—a motley collection of amateur soldiers—were crushed and dispersed as the British moved on to Concord in perfect order with their banners fluttering in the breeze and their bayonets sparkling in the morning sun.

The British found no arms at Concord. Instead, they found the rebellion they were trying to prevent.

Driven by years of unredressed grievances and shocked by the violence on the Lexington green, a thoroughly aroused populace, now vastly outnumbering the British expedition, attacked the regulars and a relief brigade sent to rescue them. Although badly mauled, the British managed to reach Charlestown. There, they crossed the Charles River and staggered into Boston—exhausted, but safe from the hordes of menacing provincials.

The American Revolution had begun.

For the next six years the war raged from Georgia to Maine as a desperate America tried to wrench herself free of colonial rule. In the end, and with the aid of France, America drove great and mighty England from her shores.

In the mind of this author, every American who actively opposed the presence of British rule in the colonies—as that rule became hard and unreasonable—was a hero. In whatever way, large or small, the thousands of patriots who pitted their lives against the power of England performed a collective act of remarkable courage.

The fifty people whose deeds are briefly described in this book—forty-five Americans and five foreign friends—represent a limited cross section of the kinds of people who risked all to move the American colonies toward sovereignty.

Some were important leaders, famous and wealthy. Others were ordinary citizens, unknown and not very rich. There were those who gave their lives and whom we shall always remember for their individual valor. There were those we recall because of what they said or wrote. Also, there were those whose names rarely appear on the pages of popular history, but who, nevertheless, are the stuff from which legends are made and about whom ballads are sung. Included too are the few who fumbled and bumbled their way into history—heroes on Sunday, fools on Monday—yet, key figures in the cause for independence.

Some of these people were, perhaps, more ambitious than they should have been—temperamental and vain. They were human and imperfect. Many were dedicated beyond their abilities—inexperienced, if not altogether incompetent. The success of such a huge and meaningful enterprise as the revolution they all waged against Great Britain was not a simple matter of clever victories here and stupid defeats there. The pressures, forces, and currents of the eighteenth-century world that moved about them were, at times, unbearable. Still, they were iron-willed, vigorous people who occupied some center stage or other, in varying degrees and in such a way that they nourished the spirit of liberty, passing it on to others.

CONTENTS

ALPHABETICAL GUIDE TO THE HEROES

I. THE NEW ENGLAND COLONIES

JOHN ADAMS 1735-1826

Not every Yankee hero of the American Revolution was a straight-shooting soldier. Some patriots helped to secure American independence without performing any acts of derring-do on the battlefield. Massachusetts lawyer John Adams was such a patriot. Destined to become second President of the United States, he argued persuasively for independence while less courageous men hoped for compromise. It was John Adams who proposed a Declaration of Independence, helped to draft the document, and finally convinced an uncertain Congress to adopt it. Again, it was John Adams who proposed that a Virginian, George Washington, be placed in command of an American army. Washington was appointed. Thus, Virginia became firmly bound to the cause of tormented Massachusetts, and all thirteen colonies were welded into a single force to deal more effectively with their common enemy, England. Although he rankled many with his impatience, suspicions, and bluntness, "Honest John" Adams challenged the repressive rule of mighty Great Britain with uncommon intellect—and won!

SAMUEL ADAMS 1722-1803

Britain's most implacable foe in America was Sam Adams, the impoverished Boston politician. Unlike his cousin John, who vigorously but politely pressed for independence in the highest councils, Sam Adams went directly to the people to preach his doctrine of violent rebellion. He stalked the streets in a stained and rumpled suit, sowing seeds of revolution. He organized youthful gangs from the North and South Ends of Boston into the Sons of Liberty to keep the passion of liberty ever alive. He inflamed people everywhere with biting articles that were distributed by a committee he himself had founded—the Committee of Correspondence. He engineered the Boston Tea Party, causing the military occupation of Boston. The British issued a warrant for his arrest but never found him. Instead of ending up with the notorious Sam Adams, the British expedition that was sent to arrest him found itself chin-high in a shooting war. Samuel Adams, the Architect of Revolution, finally had his way.

ETHAN ALLEN 1738-1789

The British bastion, Fort Ticonderoga, loomed above New York's Lake Champlain like an unconquerable sentinel. But on the night of May 10, 1775—five weeks before the Battle of Bunker Hill—its massive stones were not enough to hold back a tide of liberty-driven Yankees. On that night, the usually explosive Ethan Allen of Vermont quietly stole into the fort with 300 of his Green Mountain Boys and a detachment of Connecticut militiamen. The guards were quickly and easily overwhelmed. The sleeping British garrison awoke suddenly to find that Fort Ticonderoga belonged to the Americans. Emboldened by this bloodless victory (not a single American fell), flashy, muscular Ethan Allen aimed his Green Mountain Boys at Canada. In September, 1775, he attacked Montreal, only to be captured and sent to England. He was later returned to Canada and finally released in 1778. The following year he wrote and published a widely read account of his imprisonment, *A Narrative of Col. Ethan Allen's Captivity*.

CAPTAIN DAVID BUSHNELL 1742?-1824

It was late August, 1776. H.M.S. *Eagle,* a British man-of-war, rolled lazily in the balmy waters off Governor's Island, New York. A new day was about to dawn, clear and bright. Below the gently lapping surface of the still, dark bay, unseen by the watch on board, was the *American Turtle*—a submarine— the brainchild of a man from Saybrook, Connecticut, David Bushnell. Inside the clam-shaped machine was Ezra Lee, an American army sergeant. Lee was desperately trying to drill a hole into the copper-sheathed hull of the warship with a tool operated from inside the tiny wooden craft. Bushnell and Lee had hoped to blow up the British ship by inserting a timed torpedo into her hull. However, hampered by currents, a dull drill, and poor lever-age, Lee was unable to penetrate the metal-covered hull. With the coming of daylight, Lee feared he would be discovered and decided to withdraw. The mission failed. Nevertheless, David Bushnell did what no one had ever done before. He designed and built a practical, armed submarine that could successfully submerge and surface, and sent it to sea to sink an enemy ship.

DEBORAH GANNETT ?-?

Black American soldiers participated in nearly every battle against the British from Bunker Hill to Yorktown. Many were slaves pressed into service as valets for their battle-bound white masters. Others fought as substitutes for owners who declined to do their own fighting. Slaves from every colony joined the army on the promise that they would be given their freedom. Some black men were already freemen who voluntarily served the patriot cause. Among these was Robert Shurtliff. Shurtliff enlisted in the Fourth Massachusetts Regiment on May 20, 1782 and served without pay until October 23, 1783. Private Shurtliff's record would have gone unnoticed had it not been for the fact that the former soldier wanted to be paid—nine years later! In reviewing the petition, the General Court of Massachusetts discovered that Robert Shurtliff was, in reality, Deborah Gannett, a black woman. Miss Gannett was duly paid with interest. And for her well-disguised secret she received a citation for gallantry.

NATHANAEL GREENE 1742-1786

Nathanael Greene, a Rhode Island lawmaker, rushed to Boston soon after the fighting erupted at Lexington. There, he helped lay siege to the British garrison. When the British evacuated Boston in 1776, Greene was placed in command of the city. Later that year he was transferred to New York. At Christmastime he crossed the Delaware with George Washington to defeat the Hessians at Trenton. He then fought at Brandywine and Germantown, froze at Valley Forge, and fought again at Monmouth. He returned to New York to preside over the trial that sent British Major John André to the gallows and branded Benedict Arnold a traitor. Finally, in 1780, Greene was named to command the Southern Army. He fought Lord Cornwallis at Guilford Court House, North Carolina on March 15, 1781, and lost. However, he inflicted such heavy losses upon the British that they were forced to retire to Wilmington. Greene then drove south and surrounded Charleston, South Carolina. One month later, having failed to corner and crush the American general, Cornwallis marched northward into Virginia, where he would lose the war for Great Britain.

NATHAN HALE 1755-1776

Young Nathan Hale, a captain in the Continental Army, had just passed his twenty-first birthday when he was transferred from Boston to New York. One of a fearless company of Rangers, he was already known for his daring when he volunteered to obtain information on the enemy's strength. Masquerading as a schoolmaster, he passed easily through the British lines. This was a natural disguise for the young officer from Connecticut. He *had* been a schoolmaster for two years following his graduation from Yale College in 1773. Unfortunately, he was found out—perhaps betrayed by a Tory relative—and seized near Huntington, Long Island, September 21, 1776. He was quickly brought before General William Howe, who summarily condemned him to die. Without benefit of trial, he was taken to New York City the next day and promptly hung. Those who witnessed the execution reported that the British officer in charge denied him any last requests. With angry defiance, Nathan Hale was said to have exclaimed, "I only regret that I have but one life to lose for my country."

JOHN HANCOCK 1737-1793

John Hancock was one of Boston's vainest and wealthiest men—a merchant who inherited a great fortune upon the death of an uncle. Angered by the 1765 Stamp Tax and what he considered to be unfair restrictions on colonial commerce—chiefly his own—Hancock embarked on a career of defiance. He allowed his vessels to smuggle goods into the colonies until one of them, the *Liberty,* was seized by the British. A tumultuous riot followed the seizure. The colonists burned the ship to prevent the British from keeping her. Soon after, in 1769, Hancock was elected to the Massachusetts General Court, where he fell under the spell of Sam Adams. From that moment on, John Hancock used his money and influence to openly promote violent rebellion and his own selection as commanding general of the colonial army. The British put a price on his head. Like Sam Adams, with whom he went into hiding, Hancock escaped. He turned up later, not as a general, but as President of the Second Continental Congress and the first to sign the Declaration of Independence.

CAPTAIN JOHN PARKER 1729-1775

It was Wednesday, April 19, 1775. The sun had not yet risen. Seven hundred British troops were approaching Lexington, Massachusetts, through a hovering mist that seemed to separate night from day. They had been marching all night, northwestward from Boston, to destroy the colonial arms supply in Concord. They had arrest warrants for Sam Adams and John Hancock, who, they had reason to believe, were hiding nearby. As the first element of 400 soldiers passed the southern end of the Lexington green, their eyes fell upon a line of some thirty-five minutemen at the other end with about forty more armed men racing to join the little line formed up behind their captain, John Parker. The British ordered them to lay down their arms. They refused. The redcoats advanced. The Americans fell back. "Stand your ground," Parker barked. "Don't fire unless fired upon. If they mean to have a war, let it begin here." The American line steadied. A shot split the air. Neither side knew who had fired. Startled, the British smashed into the stubborn line of minutemen. Eight colonials died. Ten were wounded. The war did indeed begin then and there.

COLONEL WILLIAM PRESCOTT 1729-1795

British General Thomas Gage, the royal governor of Massachusetts, ordered General William Howe to take the high ground around Charlestown. Gage hoped to use this advantage to break the colonists' siege of Boston. Hearing of the plan, the Americans hastily sent Colonel William Prescott and 1500 poorly trained militiamen to occupy Charlestown's Bunker Hill. Prescott, however, decided to fortify Breed's Hill nearby, instead. The next morning, June 17, 1775, Howe crossed the Charles River with 2500 Regulars to dislodge the Americans. In the battle that followed—mistakenly called the Battle of Bunker Hill—the British were victorious, but they paid a terrible price. Twice they attacked the American positions only to be turned back. They succeeded on their third attempt when Prescott and his amateur soldiers ran out of gunpowder. Some 400 Americans were casualties that day. But more than 1000 Britons fell. News of Prescott's gallant defense spread like wildfire and stiffened American resistance everywhere.

GENERAL ISRAEL PUTNAM 1718-1790

A veteran soldier, Israel Putnam thought he had fought his last battle at Fort Detroit in 1763. He had been sent there to relieve a small British force that had been withstanding a siege led by Pontiac, the great Indian chief. Before that, Putnam had faced England's foes from Montreal to the West Indies. During the years that followed, he became active in various patriot committees and spoke out against England. However, Putnam spent most of these years working his Connecticut farm, content to leave violent patriotic outbursts to younger men. When news of the fighting at Lexington and Concord reached him, 57-year-old Israel Putnam immediately headed for Massachusetts. There—at Cambridge—"Old Put" joined in the siege of Boston as a major general. Later, he was seen as a combatant in the savage fighting on Breed's Hill, fearlessly flailing away at the oncoming British. But never again would this old soldier reach such heroic heights. Thereafter his military career was marked by blunders and ineptness as he tangled with the British in New York. He suffered a stroke in 1779 and left the war behind him.

PAUL REVERE 1735-1818

Wherever there was outdoor revolutionary work to be done, Paul Revere, the stocky Boston silversmith, could be relied upon to do it. He had dumped English tea into Boston Harbor, organized a spy network, delivered the saber-rattling Suffolk Resolves to the Continental Congress, and otherwise made himself useful. On the night of April 18, 1775—about 11 P.M.—some twenty minutes after two signal lights flickered in the steeple of Christ Church, Revere was rowed across the moon-washed Charles River to Charlestown. He landed as British troops waded ashore at Cambridge to begin their march on Concord. He mounted a waiting horse and rode to Lexington to warn Hancock and Sam Adams of the coming troops. On the way he roused the whole countryside to arms. Duly warned, Hancock and Adams fled. Revere saved Hancock's valuable papers after having been caught and released by a British patrol. A year later he entered the army and served as an artillery officer on an island in Boston Harbor. In 1779 he participated in the disastrous American expedition at Penobscot, Maine. For his part in the defeat, Revere was court-martialed. He was acquitted. Soon after, he resigned from the army.

JACK SISSON ?-?

American General Charles Lee was an English prisoner in Rhode Island. The British offered to release him if the Americans would free a captive British general. They thought the offer amusing inasmuch as the Americans held not one British general. Seeing an opportunity to embarrass their foe, the colonials decided to capture one and exchange him for Lee. Accordingly, Colonel William Barton and some volunteers set out to take General Richard Prescott, commander of the British Rhode Island army. On the dark night of July 9, 1777, they slipped into the enemy camp and came to within a mile of Prescott's quarters. From there, several of them, including Jack Sisson, a black soldier, somehow managed to reach Prescott's front door. Sisson broke it down and invaded the general's bedroom. The raiding party then forced the sleepy Prescott all the way back to the American lines—without his trousers! News of the daring, bloodless, trouserless raid sent waves of laughter rolling over England and the colonies.

GENERAL ARTEMAS WARD 1727-1800

Three days after the battle at Concord, the Massachusetts Provincial Congress elected politician Artemas Ward to head a newly authorized army. The very stout Ward, a French and Indian War veteran, knew little about commanding troops. Yet, he directed the organizing of 15,000 colonials, who had the British bottled up inside of Boston, into the appearance of an army. They built bulwarks and lay siege to the town. When the Continental Congress named Virginia's George Washington commander in chief of all colonial forces on June 15, 1775, Ward was named second in command. However, General Washington did not assume his duties until July 3. Ward was still in charge when he ordered Colonel Prescott to Bunker Hill on June 16. The result of the ensuing battle was so costly for the British, although they were victorious, that General Thomas Gage, the British commander, was recalled to Britain. The siege of Boston continued through March, 1776. Washington then fortified strategic Dorchester Heights and forced the British to evacuate Boston. Soon after, Ward resigned from the army and returned to politics.

DOCTOR JOSEPH WARREN 1741-1775

Not many believed that a lead ball tore into the handsome head of Harvard-educated Joseph Warren. But there he was—a 34-year-old newly appointed major general without a uniform, a compassionate man of medicine and principle—sprawled among the dead on Breed's Hill. The well-born physician spent ten years tormenting the British with his cunning, his speeches, his vitality, his belief in a free America, and his immense popularity. He had helped to manage the Boston Tea Party, drafted that angry prelude to the Declaration of Independence—the Suffolk Resolves, ran the revolutionary Committee of Safety as its president, relentlessly watched the British through Paul Revere's spying friends, and sent Revere and William Dawes riding off into the night to awaken the countryside as the British moved on Concord. Finally, unable to leave the fighting to others—unable to let others shed blood for a cause he helped bring to life—Joseph Warren joined the battle and died.

II. THE MIDDLE COLONIES

CAPTAIN JOHN BARRY 1745-1803

Colonial seapower consisted chiefly of an "irregular navy"—armed merchantmen, captained by fine seamen who knew nothing about naval warfare. These "privateers" sailed under no one's orders but their own. From time to time the Marine Committee of the Continental Congress had built or purchased armed vessels which it commissioned "regular navy." These ships became the responsibility of Esek Hopkins, who was appointed by a Naval Board as America's first Chief of Naval Operations. The Naval Board also commissioned a number of officers to command the ships. Among these daring "seadogs" was John Barry, a Philadelphia Irishman. He was given command of the 86-foot, 14-gun, black and yellow trimmed brig, *Lexington,* once known as the *Wild Duck.* Undaunted by British naval power, Barry took the *Lexington* to sea in 1776 and promptly captured the *Edward* after a brief skirmish. Although some British warships had been captured before—by privateers—Barry's victory marked the first time that a commissioned American warship took an enemy warship by force.

BENJAMIN FRANKLIN 1706-1790

Portly Ben Franklin, a man of mischievous wit and infinite wisdom, was one of America's most gifted citizens. Printer, author, diplomat, publisher, politician, scientist, inventor—and more—he was as much at home in the royal splendor of Paris or the civilized elegance of Georgian London as he was in the simple settings of his native land. Born into a poor Boston family, young Ben moved to Philadelphia to launch the many-sided career that brought him fame and fortune. He made frequent trips to England to represent American interests there. In London, he often protested British colonial high-handedness, while pleading for moderation among his embittered countrymen at home. His own son, William, was a Tory. When moderation failed, Franklin joined the revolution. He signed the Declaration of Independence, remarking, "We must all hang together, or assuredly we shall all hang separately." He went to Paris to charm the French into assisting the American cause and won French recognition for an independent United States of America. Finally, he laid the groundwork for a peace treaty with Great Britain.

ALEXANDER HAMILTON 1757-1804

As American and French artillery pounded Lord Cornwallis's center at Yorktown, Colonel Alexander Hamilton and his men attacked Redoubt 10—British outer defenses on the American right. A French force, meanwhile, advanced on Redoubt 9, nearby. Leading his troops recklessly over a barricade, Hamilton leaped into the British trench as his men spilled in after him. Together, with sword and fixed bayonets, they throttled the seasoned Englishmen. The French force was equally successful. The action weakened Cornwallis's left side and hastened the surrender of his outnumbered army four days later on October 18, 1781. Two and one-half months earlier, Hamilton had been George Washington's secretary. Also, he had written numerous, widely read articles that brilliantly defended the cause of independence. But the life of a staff officer and political author was not exciting enough for the lively patriot. He wanted to meet the enemy in the field and finally did. Eventually, he became America's first Secretary of the Treasury and a powerful politician. Years later he would die on a dueling field—a victim of Aaron Burr's pistol.

MARY LUDWIG HAYS 1754-1832

Everyone called her Molly. Even her husband, John Hays, called her Molly. When John went off to join General George Washington's army as an artilleryman, Molly followed him. Wherever he went, Molly seemed always to be nearby. When John Hays shivered at Valley Forge during the awful winter of 1777–78, Molly was there, too—scratching for food and trying to make herself useful. When General Washington's raggedy troops left their icy encampment at Valley Forge, Molly went with them. Finally, on the broiling hot day of June 28, 1778, the Americans caught the British at Monmouth, New Jersey. As the battle raged back and forth, Molly carried pitchers of water to the thirst-crazed colonials, including her husband. When John Hays collapsed from the terrible heat, Molly, now renamed "Molly Pitcher" by the grateful troops, ran to the side of her prostrate husband. Unable to revive him at that moment, Mary "Molly Pitcher" Hays took his position and fought in the battle as a rammer in the gun crew.

EDWARD HECTOR ?-1834

On September 11, 1777, General George Washington made a heroic effort to prevent the city of Philadelphia from falling to the British. He flung his army at the advancing redcoats and failed. The battleground— Brandywine Creek, some twenty miles south of the city—became a nightmare for the Americans. Unable to stop the British, Washington ordered a retreat. Private Edward Hector, a black volunteer in the Third Pennsylvania Artillery Regiment, was ordered to abandon his ammunition wagon. He refused to give up the precious cargo to the enemy. Instead, as the tumult exploded all around him, he slowly drove the wagon to the rear, picking up weapons dropped by the fleeing colonials. Not until the wagon sagged from the weight of the cast-off weapons did Hector leave the battlefield. He received no special recognition for this brave act. In fact, Private Hector had to wait more than fifty years for his army pay. Shortly before he died, the state of Pennsylvania paid him $40 for his part in the War for American Independence.

CAPTAIN JOHN PAUL JONES 1747-1792

His real name was John Paul. The scrappy, Scottish-born American added "Jones" in 1773 to avoid standing trial for killing a mutineer while commanding a merchantman in the Caribbean Sea. He was commissioned a lieutenant in the tiny Continental Navy in December, 1775. For three years he roamed the seas, first aboard the *Alfred,* then in command of the *Providence* and *Ranger.* He spent most of his time raiding the British coast. In 1779 he was given command of a flotilla. His flagship was the *Duc de Duras,* an old French merchantman, refitted with forty-two guns and re-named the *Bon Homme Richard.* On September 23 of that year, Jones overtook a more powerful British man-of-war, the *Serapis,* convoying some merchant-men. The *Serapis* leveled a withering fire at the oncoming American, set her aflame, ripped her from stem to stern, and asked for her surrender. "I have not yet begun to fight," Jones replied. Whereupon, he had the sinking *Bon Homme Richard* lashed to the English ship, and his crew boarded her and took her in a hand to hand, moonlit battle. It was a stunning defeat for the British—a defeat more celebrated in France, at the time, than in America.

WILLIAM LIVINGSTON 1723-1790

In September, 1774, delegates from the American colonies met in Philadelphia to decide how best to resist the tough policies of Great Britain. John Adams took note of his colleagues. Of New Jersey delegate William Livingston, Adams wrote, "He is a plain man, tall . . . nothing elegant or genteel about him." William Livingston was the youngest of three wealthy New York brothers who openly supported the patriot cause while other influential families—the De Lanceys of New York City in particular and longtime rivals of the Livingstons—supported the British. All three brothers were graduates of Yale College. Peter, the eldest, was a Whig politician. Philip was a merchant and signed the Declaration of Independence. William was New York's leading lawyer until 1772, when he moved to New Jersey. In 1776, unable to sit and talk while others stood and fought (he was not much of an orator), William Livingston resigned as a delegate to the Continental Congress in Philadelphia and went to war. He served as commander of the New Jersey militia. However, in 1777 he was elected the first governor of New Jersey under a new constitution. He remained in that office until his death.

GENERAL DANIEL MORGAN 1736-1802

Daniel Morgan began life on a New Jersey farm. While still a teen-ager, he ran away to seek a more adventurous life. He was soon caught up in frontier fighting with Indians and finally joined the British in defeating France in North America. When the American Revolution broke out, Morgan became a captain in the Continental Army. In his first campaign at Quebec, Canada, Morgan was captured after having assumed command from wounded Benedict Arnold. He was released not long after and promoted to colonel. He organized a regiment of sharpshooters that participated in numerous battles in upper New York that led to the defeat of British General Burgoyne at Saratoga. Unhappy over being unable to win further promotion, Morgan quit the army and the war. However, he returned the following year as a brigadier general and joined Horatio Gates in the Carolinas. Later, after Nathanael Greene succeeded Gates as top American commander in the South, Morgan maintained constant pressure against the British. He defeated one of Britain's most storied warriors, Sir Banastre Tarleton, at Cowpens, on January 17, 1781.

ROBERT MORRIS 1734-1806

At the age of thirteen, Robert Morris left Liverpool, England, the place of his birth, and came to Philadelphia. In the years that followed, he became an extremely successful businessman with connections in a number of the great mercantile houses of Europe. His special genius for business, handling money, and getting along with people, together with his ambitions for an independent America, made Robert Morris a valuable asset to the various patriotic committees. The hard-pressed Americans needed money and materials to support an army. They also needed friends abroad. As a delegate to the Continental Congress, Robert Morris signed the Declaration of Independence and went on working to obtain the necessary money, materials, and friends to keep the American Revolution going. In the end, after having served the new country in various financial capacities, his personal business went bankrupt. Morris was sent to debtor's prison. He languished in jail for three years from 1798 to 1801. Eventually, he died penniless and all but forgotten.

JEREMIAH O'BRIEN 1744-1818

The earliest naval engagements of the American Revolution were two battles fought between amateur seafighters. In May, 1775, patriots from the village of Machias, Maine, learned that war had broken out in Massachusetts a month before. These same patriots promptly tried to prevent the armed British schooner *Margaretta* from escorting some smaller ships to Boston with supplies for the besieged British garrison. A young New Yorker, Jeremiah O'Brien, who had been in Machias at the time, decided to get aboard one of the smaller British vessels, capture it, and then attack the *Margaretta*. With some help from the local patriots, O'Brien captured a sloop and went after the *Margaretta*. Soon after, O'Brien secured a larger ship and became a privateer. In June, 1775, O'Brien cornered two armed British schooners in Machias Harbor and defeated them. The following month he sent the captured crews to General George Washington's headquarters in Cambridge, Massachusetts. Pleased with O'Brien's success, Washington turned over the command of the captured schooners to him.

THOMAS PAINE 1737-1809

These are the times that try men's souls," wrote Thomas Paine in a pamphlet published in January, 1776. "The summer soldier and the sunshine patriot will, in this crisis, shrink from the service of his country; but he that stands it *now*, deserves the love and thanks of man and woman." The pamphlet, called *Common Sense,* was the first of many that Paine was to write during the War for Independence. His stirring words were read all over the colonies and had a great uplifting effect upon the spirit of the people and their revolution against Great Britain. Tom Paine, a former tax collector, came to America from England in 1774, one year before the outbreak of hostilities. It was not long before the fiery Englishman—once known in Britain as an agitator for higher salaries for tax collectors—became involved in the struggle for American liberty—a struggle deeply rooted in Great Britain's right to tax her colonies. In any event, Paine became famous for his frank pamphlets, all of which set forth America's case for independence and helped move the colonies closer to being a free and sovereign nation.

DOCTOR BENJAMIN RUSH 1745-1813

Doctor Benjamin Rush of Philadelphia, Pennsylvania, was one of four physicians who signed the Declaration of Independence. Lyman Hall of Georgia, Matthew Thornton and Josiah Bartlett, both of New Hampshire, were the others. The always enthusiastic Doctor Rush received his medical training in Scotland after having graduated from the College of New Jersey (now Princeton University) in 1760. Upon the completion of his studies, he returned to America—to the Philadelphia Academy—as America's first professor of chemistry. Soon, however, and like most Americans in the colonies, he was caught up in the rising tide of liberty. His political interests temporarily overtook his medical interests when he was elected a member of the Pennsylvania delegation to the Second Continental Congress. He served as a delegate until 1777. In that year he was appointed surgeon-general of the Continental Army, a post he did not keep for long. He managed to improve army medical services, but in the process unnecessarily blamed others for what he considered to be medical incompetence. An outspoken critic of General Washington, Rush unhappily resigned in 1778.

HAYM SALOMON 1740-1785

Life in a Jewish ghetto in Poland was so unbearable and unpromising that Haym Salomon decided to seek his fortune elsewhere. He arrived in New York City just as the colonies were moving toward a showdown with England. Britain's oppressive rule was nothing new to Salomon—or, for that matter, to the 2000 Jews who now lived in the colonies. With freedom uppermost in his mind, Haym Salomon became an ardent patriot and joined the Sons of Liberty. When the fighting began and English troops occupied New York, they arrested Salomon. However, being fluent in five or six languages, Salomon was released to be an interpreter for his jailer. Instead of interpreting, he helped the non-English-speaking prisoners of war escape. Soon, Salomon himself had to escape. He fled to Philadelphia, where he began a money-lending business. He became wealthy and offered his entire fortune to finance the Revolution, which was desperately in need of money and materials. With Robert Morris acting as a go-between, Salomon's money was used to pay the French troops; buy shoes, blankets, and arms for the ragtag American forces, and pay them as well. He raised other monies on his own and finally died penniless.

GENERAL PHILIP SCHUYLER 1733-1804

The career of Philip Schuyler, one of the wealthiest men in New York, ranged intermittently over the fields of politics and war. His first military service was in the French and Indian War. When it was over, he became a commissioner to settle a boundary dispute between New York and New Hampshire. His favoring of the New York position in the dispute caused him to be greatly mistrusted by Ethan Allen and his New Hampshire Green Mountain Boys. Nevertheless, after serving in the First Continental Congress, Schuyler became a general in command of the Northern Department—a sector in which the Green Mountain Boys did much of their fighting. Forgetting, temporarily, their past differences, the two patriot leaders joined forces to plan the Quebec campaign. Later, when the British retook Fort Ticonderoga, Schuyler was court-martialed for negligence. He was declared innocent but resigned from the army. He returned to the Continental Congress as a delegate from New York to continue the fight for independence.

GENERAL ANTHONY WAYNE 1745-1796

His fellow officers called him "Mad Anthony" because of his violent nature. Nevertheless, Pennsylvania-born Anthony Wayne, impetuous though he was, remained a cool officer in battle. A patriot from the beginning, Wayne was a member of the Pennsylvania Committee of Safety. With the outbreak of war, he organized a regiment and was commissioned a colonel in the Continental Army. He covered the American retreat at Quebec and was promoted to brigadier general. He led a brigade at Brandywine and lost at Paoli in Pennsylvania. He was court-martialed for the "Paoli Massacre" losses but acquitted. Wayne then went on to fight the British to a standstill at Germantown. When the Americans retired to Valley Forge, Wayne kept them supplied by steadily raiding the nearby British. He fought in the blistering battle of Monmouth and later trounced the British at Stony Point on the Hudson River. He went south and occupied Charleston, South Carolina and then turned north to participate in the Yorktown campaign. Eventually, in 1792, Anthony Wayne became commander in chief of the American army and led an expedition to the Northwest Territory, where he defeated the Indians.

III. THE SOUTHERN COLONIES

COLONEL GEORGE ROGERS CLARK 1752-1818

Virginia-born George Rogers Clark spent most of the Revolutionary War years fighting the British and their Indian allies in the lands west of Virginia. Between 1776 and 1778, Clark crisscrossed the Kentucky region defending colonial settlements from English-inspired Indian attacks. Frustrated by the strain of continuous defensive battles, Clark decided that the only way to rid the area of the enemy was to go on the offensive. But he needed an army for the job rather than the overworked bands of sharpshooting settlers. In 1778 he convinced Governor Patrick Henry of Virginia to send an expedition into the western lands. With Colonel Clark in command, the expedition captured a number of British strongholds, including Vincennes in the Illinois territory. When Clark moved on, the British retook Vincennes, where they were trapped by terrible winter floods. Braving unbelievable hardships, Clark's army returned to Vincennes in February, 1779, and routed the British. He continued to attack the British-Indian forces in the west and brought much of that region under American control.

AUSTIN DABNEY ?-?

When Savannah, Georgia, fell to the British in December, 1778, it became clear to the colonial command that the entire South was in danger of being overrun. Indeed, by the end of 1779, nearly all of Georgia was in British hands. The fall of Savannah did not diminish the colonists' will to fight on, however. A number of Georgia battles took place during the first weeks of 1779. Among these was a battle fought around Kettle Creek. Wounded in that fight was Austin Dabney, a veteran Negro artilleryman. Dabney's career as a soldier was typical of the many black men who fought for American independence. A Burke County slave, Dabney enlisted in the army to obtain his personal freedom. The full meaning of "liberty" was not lost on the former slave. Yet, it took forty-two years for Dabney's courage under fire to be recognized. In 1821, the state of Georgia cited Austin Dabney for bravery in the Battle of Kettle Creek and awarded him about 100 acres of land. The federal government also voted him a yearly pension.

GENERAL HORATIO GATES 1727-1806

British general John Burgoyne went down to defeat before Horatio Gates at Saratoga, New York, in October, 1777. The stunning American victory made Gates, a former career officer in the British army, an overnight hero. Horatio Gates had first come to America in the 1750s to fight in the French and Indian War. When peace came, he returned to England and left the army. In 1772, he came back to America to settle some lands in western Virginia. An avid patriot, he was commissioned a general in the American army at the outset of the Revolution. He served near Boston until the campaign in upper New York got under way. Some political leaders and army officers tried to have Gates replace George Washington as commander in chief. The plan—known as the Conway Cabal—failed. Instead, Gates was appointed president of the War Board, a committee that managed military affairs. When, in 1780, Cornwallis threatened to overwhelm the South, Gates was sent to stop him. At Camden, South Carolina, Gates's poorly equipped and poorly trained troops were almost annihilated by the British. As the disaster unfolded, Gates fled the battle with his staff. Once a hero, Gates became a disgrace.

PATRICK HENRY 1736-1799

Between 1765 and 1774, Patrick Henry sat in the Virginia House of Burgesses and baited the British Empire with his golden tongue. "If this be treason," he remarked, "Make the most of it." Patrick Henry was the orator of the rebellion. There was no one to equal him. The words of this fiery lawyer rolled over the colonies like claps of thunder. "Is life so dear, or peace so sweet," he declared in March, 1775, "as to be purchased at the price of chains and slavery? Forbid it, Almighty God! I know not what course others may take, but as for me, give me liberty or give me death!" In 1776, he became governor of Virginia after having served in the Continental Congress and, briefly, as commander in chief of the Virginia militia. He remained as Virginia's chief executive until 1779, working for independence and speaking out for individual liberties. His voice was the rallying cry that welded thirteen separate colonies into one nation. "I am not a Virginian," he exclaimed, "but an American." There were few who did not like what they heard.

THOMAS JEFFERSON 1743-1826

After the American Revolution had ended, Thomas Jefferson, not yet third president of the United States, wrote, "I have sworn upon the altar of God, eternal hostility against every form of tyranny over the mind of man." For the wealthy, learned Virginia-born lawyer, these were not idle words. Over and over again, before and during the Revolution—as a member of the House of Burgesses, the rebel Committee of Correspondence, the Continental Congress, or as Virginia's second governor—Jefferson denounced British authority over the colonies and those who would replace it with an American rule of the privileged few. He used his pen with extraordinary eloquence and statesmanship to assert the idea that the majority—the people themselves—had the right to govern themselves. And if they did not have the ability to do so, then they must be freely educated to achieve such responsibility. Jefferson made clear this democratic principle when, as a delegate to the Second Continental Congress, he drafted the one document that expressed and continues to express the aspirations of all Americans—the Declaration of Independence.

HENRY LAURENS 1724-1792

Heeding loud colonial protests over "taxation without representation," the English parliament repealed the Stamp Act of 1765 one year after it had become law. Parliament was still determined to exact revenue from the American colonists, however. In 1767, she imposed new customs duties—the Townshend Acts—on a variety of goods imported by the colonists. Henry Laurens, a rich South Carolina planter and merchant, once willing to live with the Stamp Act, now exploded in fury against the new taxes. He refused to pay the duties and had several of his ships seized. The Townshend Acts were repealed in 1770—chiefly because of an American boycott on British goods—and Laurens, still angry, went to England. There, he stirred up sympathy for the colonies among the English themselves. He returned home in 1774 to become a delegate to the Continental Congress. He was elected president of that body three years later. In 1780, while on a mission to conclude a treaty with Holland, Laurens was captured at sea by the British. He was thrown into the Tower of London. When the war was over, he was exchanged for Lord Cornwallis.

COLONEL HENRY LEE 1756-1818

The Lees of Virginia were one of that colony's most distinguished families. Two of them, Richard Henry Lee and his younger brother, Francis Lightfoot Lee, signed the Declaration of Independence. Another relative, Henry Lee, joined the revolt on the battlefield. Henry Lee, who would one day become the father of Confederate general Robert E. Lee, was appointed captain of a Virginia cavalry company in 1776. Three years later, as a major in command of a dashing cavalry unit called Lee's Legion, he led a lightning-like raid on the British fort at Paulus Hook—now Jersey City, New Jersey—and captured it. His daring brought him a southern assignment, notably in the Carolinas. There, while under the command of General Nathanael Greene, he executed a series of breathtaking cavalry raids during the waning years of the war that earned him the nickname, "Light-Horse Harry." It was Henry Lee, who, upon the death of George Washington in 1799, described him as "first in war, first in peace, first in the hearts of his countrymen."

RICHARD HENRY LEE 1732-1794

Richard Henry Lee was the oldest of four brothers, each of whom actively opposed Great Britain. William and Arthur Lee worked abroad as agents for the Continental Congress. Richard and Francis led Virginia's opposition to the British at home. But it remained for Richard Henry Lee to provide the strong leadership that set in motion Virginia's resolve to seek independence. Moreover, it was Richard Henry Lee who, as a delegate to the Continental Congress in Philadelphia, offered the resolution that wrenched America free of her British bonds. On June 7, 1776, he rose before his congressional colleagues and made a simple motion. "Resolved," he said, "that these United Colonies are, and of right ought to be, free and independent States, that they are absolved from all allegiance to the British Crown, and that all political connections between them and the State of Great Britain is, and ought to be totally dissolved." The momentous resolution was adopted on July 2. And on July 4, 1776, America dissolved those connections, declaring herself a sovereign nation.

FRANCIS MARION 1732?-1795

On August 16, 1780, American forces were badly beaten by the British at Camden, South Carolina. Horatio Gates, the American commander, had fled the field, leaving his troops in the charge of Johann de Kalb, a German soldier of fortune. De Kalb was mortally wounded in the action. It appeared to Lord Cornwallis, the British commander, that he had destroyed all patriot resistance in the Carolinas. He had overlooked the veteran Indian fighter, Francis Marion, however. Marion and his men knew the backcountry, with its trails and swamps, better than any English soldier in the area. He took his cavalry troopers, who had remained unscathed after the Camden defeat, into this remote country. From there, Francis Marion sallied forth, time and again, to hit the English where they least expected it and then retired to his swampy campsites before the British could retaliate. Cornwallis never knew exactly how to counteract the hit-and-run tactics of Marion's guerrillas. Marion was so cleverly elusive that he came to be known as the "Swamp Fox."

SAUL MATTHEWS ?-?

In June, 1775, the Virginia patriots forced the British royal governor, John Murray, Fourth Earl of Dunmore, to flee. Murray sought safety aboard a British ship, still determined to hold Virginia for Great Britain. On November 7, 1775, he issued a proclamation offering freedom to all black slaves if they would bear arms for England. A number of Virginia slaves responded to Murray's offer. Saul Matthews, a slave from Norfolk County, did not. Matthews joined the patriots. For six years he shouldered his musket for the cause of independence. Finally, as the war was drawing to a close, Matthews was sent into the British lines at Portsmouth, Virginia, to collect information about the British position. Remaining undetected, Matthews uncovered valuable intelligence. He followed this mission by leading a raiding party back into Portsmouth, capturing a number of prisoners. Saul Matthews was rewarded for his war service in 1792 when the state of Virginia cited him for bravery and gave him his freedom.

GENERAL WILLIAM MOULTRIE 1731-1805

William Moultrie was born in Charleston, South Carolina. And it was in his native city that Moultrie won his greatest victory and suffered his worst humiliation. Moultrie was a member of the South Carolina assembly when the revolution exploded. Immediately, he joined the Continental Army and was assigned to the command of a fort on Sullivan's Island in Charleston Harbor. On June 28, 1776, the British began an attack on Charleston by bombarding Sullivan's Island. Moultrie's garrison withstood the severe pounding. Their stubborn defense prevented the British from continuing the attack and capturing Charleston. Moultrie was quickly promoted to brigadier general. Three years later, he caught the British at Beaufort, a coastal town south of Charleston, and defeated them. By 1780, the American position in the Deep South had become desperate, however. In the spring of that year, Sir Henry Clinton, the British general, attacked Charleston. Surrounded and overwhelmed by superior forces, the city surrendered. Among the American prisoners was General William Moultrie.

ANDREW PICKENS 1739-1817

Andrew Pickens had come to South Carolina from Pennsylvania in the 1750s. Some ten years later, he was embroiled in the frontier fighting that saw many a South Carolinian battling the Cherokee Indians. Like Francis Marion, the "Swamp Fox," Pickens learned then and there the stealthy tactics that he would use to sting the British in the Carolina campaign of the American Revolution. After the Battle of Camden in August, 1780, the badly mauled Americans were unable to effectively resist British control of the Carolinas. Patriot Andrew Pickens was unwilling to let the British have it all their way. Like Francis Marion, he organized his own band of guerrilla fighters and repeatedly kept the British off balance by harassing their lines. When General Nathanael Greene finally reorganized the American southern forces, Pickens and his tough guerrillas joined him. Together, they fought a series of engagements in 1781—including the Battles of Cowpens, Augusta, and Eutaw Springs—that eventually led to the total defeat of Great Britain.

FRANCIS SALVADOR ?-1776

The Jewish community in America did not number much more than 2000 persons when the War for Independence began. Like every other group in the colonies, there were those among them who remained loyal to the crown and those who cast their lot with the rebels. Francis Salvador, a young Jewish aristocrat who had left his London home in 1773 for Charleston, South Carolina, put himself squarely on the side of the patriots. By 1775, he was a member of South Carolina's rebellious Provincial Congress. When a British fleet attacked Charleston in June, 1776 and the Cherokees invaded South Carolina on the side of the English, Salvador joined the fight. On August 1, 1776, Salvador was riding with a detachment of the South Carolina militia when it was ambushed by a force of Tories and Indians. Salvador was shot and fell from his horse. Immediately, he was set upon by some Indians and scalped. The patriots drove off their attackers. But Francis Salvador died in the arms of his friend, Major Andrew Williamson, commander of the detachment and a member of South Carolina's Provincial Congress.

GENERAL THOMAS SUMTER 1734-1832

Like Francis Marion and Andrew Pickens, Thomas Sumter was the leader of a band of Carolina irregulars or guerrillas. And like his partisan comrades, Sumter took up the resistance after the regular American forces were decisively beaten at Camden, South Carolina in 1780. Also, like Marion and Pickens, Sumter learned his brand of fighting on the American frontier. He left his Virginia home in 1755 to fight the French and Indians under General Edward Braddock. He participated in the British disaster at Fort Duquesne (now Pittsburgh, Pennsylvania), where Braddock lost his life. He returned to Fort Duquesne several years later with General Edward Forbes to rout the French. He battled the Cherokees before trying to settle down as a South Carolina planter. During most of the Carolina campaign, Thomas Sumter used the frontier skills he had learned so well to torment the British. He and Sir Banastre Tarleton, the British cavalry officer, pecked away at each other in a seemingly endless series of confrontations. For his part, Sumter was so reckless and ferocious that he became known as the "Gamecock."

GENERAL GEORGE WASHINGTON 1732-1799

No man in colonial America was faced with a more impossible task than the tall Virginia aristocrat, George Washington, commander in chief of the Continental Army. When he assumed command on July 3, 1775, he had not led troops for twenty years. His last experience had been against the French and Indians at Fort Duquesne in 1755. Moreover, his new army was not an army at all, but a gathering of 15,000 armed civilians. Washington had to forge a regular army from that motley collection of Americans and then use it to beat one of the world's mightiest military powers— England. Everyone knew that the revolution could not be won with oratory and resolutions. It had to be won on the battlefield. And George Washington was charged with the responsibility of doing just that. For six years he labored through great defeats, small victories, mutinies, treacheries, and unspeakable hardships. But with stubborn dedication, personal strength and wisdom, George Washington was able to keep his tattered troops together and finally drive England from the American colonies.

IV. FOREIGN ALLIES

HENRI CHRISTOPHE 1767-1820

Savannah, Georgia fell to the British on December 29, 1778. Less than a year later, in September, 1779, the Americans and their French allies tried to retake the city. A fleet under the command of French admiral Charles Hector, Comte d'Estaing, arrived in Savannah waters with a combined French-American army. Included in the assault force were some 500 free Negroes from Haiti, a French possession in the West Indies. Among these black troops was a sergeant who would one day become Emperor of Haiti— Henri Christophe. On October 9, 1779, having failed to bring Savannah to her knees with a naval bombardment, d'Estaing ordered his troops to storm the city. Sergeant Christophe's unit was one of the first to land. Almost immediately, a savage British counterattack drove the allies back. Christophe and his detachment formed a rear guard and held the British long enough to prevent the complete annihilation of the Franco-American force. The British held Savannah that day. But Henri Christophe, wounded in the battle, was cited for his bravery.

MARQUIS DE LAFAYETTE 1757-1834

Marie Joseph Paul Yves Roch Gilbert du Motier, Marquis de Lafayette, came from one of France's most notable families. Yet, his royal blood did not prevent him from championing the cause of American liberty. Although the French government maintained a position of strict neutrality when the American Revolution began, Lafayette was able to obtain permission to join the colonial American army. The Continental Congress made him a general upon his arrival in Philadelphia in 1777. Soon after receiving his American commission, the young marquis was wounded at the Battle of Brandywine and went into the miserable winter retreat at Valley Forge. He and General Washington became fast friends during that awful winter of 1777–78. Finally, Lafayette's own country sent a fleet to aid the Americans. But it was not enough. Lafayette traveled to France in 1779, remaining there for a year to plead for more assistance for his embattled American comrades. He returned to America in time to participate in the Yorktown battles that brought defeat to England.

COUNT CASIMIR PULASKI 1748?-1779

Having escaped from one revolution in his native Poland—a revolt which he had helped to foment—Count Casimir Pulaski joined another rebellion, the American Revolution. Armed with a letter from Benjamin Franklin which he had obtained in Paris, Pulaski came to America in 1777 and sought out George Washington. Suitably impressed, General Washington had Pulaski commissioned a brigadier general. The count then led a cavalry unit at the Battles of Brandywine and Germantown before allowing the temper tantrums of "Mad Anthony" Wayne, his immediate superior, to unsettle him. Pulaski refused to serve under Wayne. He quit the army but not the Revolution. The count turned up as leader of his own cavalry and infantry force, the Pulaski Legion. Pulaski's Legion fought in numerous engagements as a Polish ally of the Continental army. When French admiral d'Estaing stormed Savannah, Georgia on October 9, 1779, Pulaski's Legion was in the thick of the fight. The count himself led a charge in that ill-fated expedition and was mortally wounded. He died two days later.

COMTE DE ROCHAMBEAU 1725-1807

In 1780, King Louis XVI of France sent Comte de Rochambeau and a 6000-man army to aid the Americans. Like Lafayette, Jean Baptiste Donatien de Vimeur, Comte de Rochambeau, was a French nobleman. Also, he was a professional soldier with vast experience. But unlike Lafayette, Rochambeau did not march onto the battlefield immediately. His troops remained for the better part of a year in Rhode Island. During this period, British general Cornwallis had moved his army onto the Yorktown peninsula in Virginia. The Americans now saw a way to trap him. Late in the summer of 1781, at Rochambeau's urging, a French fleet under Admiral de Grasse sailed up from the West Indies and landed 3000 French marines near Cornwallis. While Lafayette waited with more troops south of Yorktown, Rochambeau joined Washington in New York. Bypassing New York City—a move unexpected by the British—they marched to Yorktown. For three weeks in October, 1781, the Franco-American army pounded the cornered, outnumbered British while the French fleet kept British reinforcements from interfering. Finally, on October 19, Cornwallis surrendered. The war for American independence was over.

BARON FRIEDRICH VON STEUBEN 1730-1794

George Washington's Continental Army was largely a collection of ill-trained, undisciplined, amateur soldiers until Friedrich Wilhelm von Steuben appeared on the scene. Von Steuben was a Prussian regular army officer and an aide to Frederick the Great, the German Emperor. Moreover, he was a recognized expert on military discipline. In 1777, while in Paris, France, Von Steuben was approached by American agents who asked him to come to America and train the army. Von Steuben agreed. He received a commission as general. Soon after his arrival in the colonies, the Prussian found himself sharing the misery of the unhappy American troops at Valley Forge, Pennsylvania. Taking advantage of the lull in fighting, disregarding the shivering complaints and the deadly winter, Von Steuben began his lessons in basic discipline. He drilled the cold and tattered troops from dawn to dusk and turned them into a tough, spirited fighting force. More than that, however, Von Steuben restored their morale. By the spring of 1778, he had given George Washington's army at Valley Forge the will to fight on.